Slow Cooker Made Easy...

Paul Brodel & Dee Hunwicks
Introduction

Welcome to the world of the Slow Cooker! Cooking food over a long period is not a new concept: people have been cooking this way for many years. But why do you need one? Well, as you explore this book you will see how slow cooking has evolved for the 21st century.

A Slow Cooker is a must in every home; it saves time, energy and gives you the convenience of a delicious meal cooked for hours and prepared in minutes. You can make quick meals with just four minutes preparation, suet pie dishes, dinner party dishes, large family meals... in fact you can cook just about anything you want. As with our other successful "Made Simple" cookbooks, each recipe has a clear step-by-step guide and is crammed full of photos.

Explore the pages and discover how you can save money by buying cheaper cuts of meat without sacrificing taste or tenderness. As always, the recipes are not set in stone. If you don't have an ingredient, it's not a problem. Just use what you do have. You won't be disappointed.

After you have used your Slow Cooker, you will wonder how you managed before, so sit back and enjoy the free time it gives you. The Slow Cooker allows you to bulk cook and freeze and is versatile enough to let you make soup, pot roasts, chilli con carnes, curries and even steam puddings, cakes and creme caramel all with minimal preparation time and maximum results.

You can even use your Slow Cooker for buffets or barbecues as they can keep your precooked or barbecued food warm, which means no more burnt sausages!

Slow Cooking - A Beginner's Guide.

This cookbook was aimed to give you ideas so you can put together a meal quickly in the mornings or lunch time and come home to a delicious evening meal without having to do much work. We have also created recipes that you might not normally do in a Slow Cooker.

The Science

The Slow Cooker uses a small amount of energy to heat the cooking pot to a temperature just below boiling point so that you can cook slowly over a long period of time. This means that if you are busy and need to leave serving until later you can generally allow an extended cooking time without the risk of ruining your dish.

Please remember all times are approximate and food should be thoroughly cooked before eating.

The Slow Cookers

We used four different Slow Cookers that ranged in size:

1½ litre 150 watts Crock Pot (2 portion)
3½ litre 160 watts Crock Pot (4 portion)
5½ litre 240 watts glass Slow Cooker* (4-6 portion)
6½ litre 375 watts (6-8 portion)
* (The glass bowl Slow Cooker was the easiest to clean)
All of the Slow Cookers we used worked very well.

Rough Guide To Cooking Times - varies by size of Slow Cooker.

High (97° C average temp) = 5-6 hours
Low (93° C average temp) = 8-9 hours
Auto (high to start then reducing to 93° C average temp) = 7-8 hours
Most of our recipes are cooked on high. If you want to use the low setting then generally you should add 2 hours to your cooking time and 1 hour when using the auto setting, ensure the food is cooked before eating.

Adapting the recipes to a Compact Oven or Regular Oven

The compact oven we used had a temperature setting of 153°C with a 2ltr cooking oven dish and the oven was sealed so no moisture could escape. If yours is open you may, depending on the recipe, wish to cover the oven dish in tin foil. When referring to the crock pot, you will use an oven dish instead. There is also no need to preheat the oven dish with boiling water. Your compact oven may have a variable temperature, if so then work on the 153°C temperature on a basic oven function, (this can also be applied to a regular oven). Also make sure that whichever oven dish your using that it has at least a 2ltr capacity.

Precautions When Using A Slow Cooker

- Always check that food is thoroughly cooked before eating.
- Never cook meat from frozen in the Slow Cooker.
- To avoid thermal shock, do not put ice cold items in an empty, hot Slow Cooker. Always heat with a little water. This stops it getting too hot, as water only boils at 100° C.
- Always refer to the manufacturers' instructions.
- There are some quick preparation recipes where we have timed the preparation to be approximately 4 minutes or less. This does not include time taken to wash the vegetables.
- Always wear oven gloves/mitts when handling the hot Crock Pot during and after cooking. Remember it will stay hot for some time.
- Only ever put food in the Crock Pot, NEVER put food or liquid in the body of the Slow Cooker.

Benefits Of Using A Slow Cooker

Cooking over a long period of time helps to tenderise meat so you can use cheaper cuts that normally have a lot more flavour. Unlike an oven (where you need to heat a large volume and use much higher temperatures to do so) the Slow Cooker has a smaller volume to heat and uses a lower temperature for cooking so it is more economical to run.

Use your Slow Cooker instead of your oven

To cook a chilli it takes about the same amount of time as in the oven - about 2 hours 35 minutes - however the advantage is that the Slow Cooker uses less energy which saves you money.

When cooking a curry or casserole, for example, seal the meat in a frying pan and add sauces or liquid, bring to temperature then pour into the preheated Crock Pot (preheat it by rinsing with warm water, then drying off the outside, then put back into the Slow Cooker body) and set the Slow Cooker to high.

We hope this book shows you how simple and easy slow cooking can be and gives you plenty of ideas for a variety of foods from soups to Christmas pudding. Happy Cooking!

We state which size slow cooker we used in each recipe if yours is a different size then adjust the recipe accordingly so the ingredients fit. You can cook a smaller amount in a larger slow cooker it doesn't have to be full.

Top Tips When Cooking With Slow Cookers

- Wipe the inner sides of the Crock Pot with vegetable oil before cooking. This will help to prevent any foods/liquids sticking to the sides.

- We found it better to thicken recipes at the end of the cooking time. This reduces the chance of ingredients sticking to the edge during cooking.

- We recommend washing your Crock Pot with warm water (and dry the outside) before you begin. This will help it to heat up faster.

- When choosing your Slow Cooker it is often better to choose a slightly larger one than you think you need because:
  a. You can always do less in a large one, but not more in a small one.
  b. You can bulk cook and freeze which can be far more cost effective.
  c. Vegetables can fit around a joint when cooking.

- We tried pasta dishes, but did not include the recipes, as we weren't wholly satisfied with the results. If you really want to cook with pasta, our only tip is to use a whole wheat variety as this will stay together longer.

- Take care with rice dishes. Monitor them, make sure you stir them occasionally and be careful not to let them overcook.

- Always pre-boil any ham joints in water for about 30 minutes before you slow cook. This lowers the salt content.

- When cooking vegetables with a joint of meat:
  - Leave skins on potatoes to keep flavour sealed in.
  - Carrots, parsnips, swede and turnip can be peeled but left whole.

- As a rule, broccoli and other green vegetables tend to go mushy, so steam them separately for optimum results.

- Always take care when removing a hot Crock Pot and use oven gloves.

Stocks

Slow Cookers are great for making tasty, wholesome, clear stock. We use three main types of stock; chicken, beef and fish. These stock recipes can be varied to your own preference.

Chicken Stock

Chicken bones from a chicken carcass
1 celery stalk or 1/4 tsp celery seeds
7 peppercorns
3 bay leaves
1 tsp mixed herbs or bouquet garni
1 onion (peeled and halved)
2 to 3 litres boiling water
2 carrots (peeled)
1 swede (peeled) optional
(add for a couple hours then remove)
1 leek (trimmed)
Parsley sprigs (or a pinch of dried)
Add giblets to make a richer stock
Season with salt and pepper

Beef Stock

Beef bones (browned using a little oil in a frying pan)
1 onion (peeled and halved)
1 carrot (peeled and halved)
1 celery stalk
1 parsley sprig (or a pinch of dried)
1 bay leaf
6 peppercorns
1 blade black mace (optional)
Mixed dried herbs (or bouquet garni)
2 to 3 litres boiling water
Season with salt and pepper

Slow cook all stock ingredients on high setting with the lid on for 6-10 hours skimming when needed to remove froth and fat.
Sieve and use when cooking soup, casserole, gravy, curry, sauces etc.

We do not recommend making stock in a compact oven.

Fish Stock

½ kilo fish trimmings (heads, tails, fins, etc)
1 onion (peeled and halved)
1 celery stalk or ¼ tsp celery seeds
Parsley sprigs (or ¼ tsp dried parsley)
2 bay leaves
7 peppercorns
½ tsp mixed herbs or bouquet garni
250 ml white wine
¼ tsp granulated sugar
Pinch of salt and white pepper

Slow cook all stock ingredients on high with lid on for 6 to 10 hours skimming when needed to remove excess froth and fat. Sieve and use in cooking. ***We do not recommend making fish stock in a compact oven.***

Poached Eggs

Run the bowl from your Slow Cooker under a warm tap, dry and replace, then turn the Slow Cooker to high. Carefully pour boiling water into the Crock Pot until the water is approximately 2 inches from the bottom. Gently crack the eggs (individually) into the water. You can crack the egg into a cup first then gently tip into the water. Replace the lid and cook for 15-30 minutes depending how well done you like them cooked. Eggs at room temperature will cook quicker than straight from the fridge.
For use with a compact oven follow the above cooking method and cook for 15-20 minutes at 153°C in only half the amount of water.

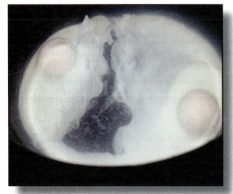  

Poached Salmon

Ingredients

Salmon fillets
Seasoning Options:
Bay leaves
Peppercorns
2 tbsp white wine
1 tbsp wine vinegar
Herbs (dried)
5g butter
1 lemon wedge

Method

Pre-warm the Crock Pot with warm/hot water, empty the water and dry the outside, add 2 inches of boiling water then set to high. Make a tin foil strap by folding over a square piece of tin foil three times. Place the fish on the strap and lower into the water, then add preferred seasoning. Cook for 20-50 minutes with the lid on. Cooking time depends on size /thickness of fish. Ensure all food is cooked thoroughly before serving.

This is a gentle way of cooking your fish.

For use with a compact oven follow the above cooking method and cook for 15-20 minutes at 153°C in only half the amount of water.

Rice Cooker

Run the Crock Pot from your Slow Cooker under a warm tap, dry and replace. Turn the Slow Cooker onto high. Add one cup of rice to every two cups of boiling water and leave to cook for 1-1½ hours depending on the power of your Slow Cooker. You will have perfect rice every time.

For use in compact oven, follow the above cooking method and cook for 15- 25 minutes at 153°C. Then add one cup of rice to two cups of boiling water and up the amount accordingly.

CONTENTS / INDEX

Starters / Appetisers:

PAGE

Main Courses / Entrée:

Main Courses / Entrée: (Continued)

Desserts:

Q = Quick to prepare recipes, prepared in less than 4 minutes once all of the vegetables have been washed.

Bacon & Bean Soup

Ingredients

2 x 400g/16oz tins mixed beans (in sauce)
4 rashers streaky or back bacon (chopped)
1 litre/40fl oz chicken stock
2 large potatoes (cubed)
1 sweet potato (cubed)
125g/5oz red lentils
75g/3oz pearl barley
1 x 400g/16oz tin chopped tomatoes
1 large onion (diced)
1 tsp garlic paste (optional)
Salt and pepper to taste
Garnish
Fresh parsley
Serve with crusty bread.

Serves 4-6
(6½ litre slow cooker was used)

Method

1. Turn the Slow Cooker onto high.
2. Place the beans, bacon, chicken stock, potatoes, sweet potato, red lentils, pearl barley, chopped tomatoes, onion and garlic paste into the Slow Cooker, then season.
3. Cook for 4 hours with the lid on, stirring hourly.
4. Remove and serve with crusty bread and garnish with fresh parsley.

For use with a compact oven halve the amount of ingredients, follow the above cooking method and cook for 2 hours at 153°C (serves 2-3).

13

Chorizo and Potato Soup

Ingredients

150g/6oz chorizo sausages (diced)
3 potatoes (cubed)
1 large onion (chopped)
Salt and pepper to taste
1½ litres/60fl oz chicken stock
75g/3oz frozen peas
50ml/2fl oz double cream
1 tsp garlic paste
½ tsp mixed dried herbs
Garnish
Croutons
Serves 4-6
(6½ litre slow cooker was used)

Method

1. Turn the Slow Cooker onto high.
2. Place sausages, potatoes, onions, chicken stock, peas, garlic, mixed herbs into Slow Cooker, mix well.
3. Cook for 5 hours with lid on. At the end of cooking time, add the cream, stir in well and season.
4. Serve with croutons.

For use with a compact oven halve the amount of ingredients, follow the above cooking method and cook for 2 hours at 153°C (serves 2-3).

15

French Onion Soup

Ingredients

Soup Ingredients
6 onions (sliced)
1¼ litres/50fl oz hot beef stock
¼ tbsp butter
¼ tbsp vegetable oil
1 tbsp brown sugar
75g/3oz bread crumbs
2 garlic cloves (finely chopped)
Crouton Ingredients
½ French stick
2 tbsp mayonnaise
200g/8oz Gruyère cheese (grated)
Salt and pepper to taste
Garnish
1 tbsp fresh parsley
Serves 6
(3½ litre slow cooker was used)

Method

1. Rinse Crock Pot under a hot tap to warm, dry the outside and return to Slow Cooker. Pour in beef stock, set to high and put lid on.
2. Fry onions and garlic in a frying pan with the butter and oil for 5 minutes stirring all the time, then add to the Slow Cooker.
3. Add the bread crumbs and sugar.
4. Cook for 4 to 5 hours on high, with lid on.
5. When ready to serve, cut the French bread into slices, brush with mayonnaise and cover with Gruyère cheese, then place under a grill to brown.
6. Serve soup with a large crouton and garnish with fresh parsley.

For use with a compact oven halve the amount of ingredients, follow the above cooking method and cook for 2 hours at 153°C (serves 3).

17

Ham and Butter Bean Soup

Ingredients
120g/4¾ oz cubed ham
2 tins butter beans (drained)
2 potatoes (peeled and cubed)
1½ litres/60fl oz chicken stock
(made with 1½ stock cubes, 1 tsp white sugar)
1 tomato (diced)
1 yellow pepper (sliced)
25g/1oz butter
¼ tsp dried mixed herbs
White pepper to taste
Garnish
Parsley
½ the tomatoes and peppers
 (from ingredients list)
Serve with crusty bread
Serves 4-6
(5½ litre slow cooker was used)

Method

1. Set the Slow Cooker to high.
2. Place the ham, butter beans, potatoes, chicken stock, butter, ½ tomato, ½ yellow pepper and the mixed herbs into the Crock pot and cook for 5 hours with the lid on.
3. Remove, season to taste and serve with crusty bread and garnish with the remaining tomatoes, peppers and parsley.

For use with a compact oven halve the amount of ingredients, follow the above cooking method and cook for 2 hours at 153°C (serves 2-3).

19

Apple and Cider Pork

Ingredients

2 apples (peeled, cored and diced)
225ml/9fl oz apple cider
4 pork chops or pork steaks
1 onion (finely chopped)
½ tbsp brown sugar
4 tbsp apple sauce
1 garlic clove (finely chopped)
½ tsp mixed herbs
1 tbsp cornflour

Garnish
Parsley
Serve with mashed potatoes
and steamed vegetables.
Serves 4
(5½ litre slow cooker was used)

Method

1. Set Slow Cooker to high.
2. Place apples, cider, pork, onions, brown sugar, apple sauce, garlic and mixed herbs into the Crock pot. Mix well and cook for 5 hours with the lid on.
3. Towards the end of the cooking time, mix the cornflour with a little cold water and add to the Crock Pot. Stir well and allow to thicken.
4. Serve with mashed potato and steamed vegetables, then garnish with parsley. Season to taste.

For use with a compact oven follow the above cooking method and cook for 2 hours at 153°C adding the cornflour 20 minutes before the end of cooking (serves 4).

21

BBQ Chicken and Rib Combo

Ingredients

12 chicken wings
1 rack of ribs
2 tbsp cider vinegar
1 tbsp soft dark brown sugar
2 tbsp honey
5 tbsp BBQ sauce
4 tbsp tomato sauce
1 tbsp tomato puree
1½ tsp garlic paste
2 tbsp soy sauce
Serve as combo meal with corn on the cob, mashed potato or fries.
Serves 4-6

Method

1. Place the ribs into a large pan of boiling water and boil for 30 minutes to tenderise the ribs and reduce the fat.
2. Add the chicken and continue for another 15 minutes.
3. Drain the excess water and leave until meat is dry - approximately 2 minutes
4. Mix together the vinegar, brown sugar, honey, BBQ sauce, tomato sauce, tomato purée, garlic paste and soy sauce in a large bowl.
5. Place the ribs and wings into this mixture and coat well.
6. Add 4 tbsp of water into the Crock Pot and set the Slow Cooker to high.
7. Add the whole mixture to the Crock Pot including any sauce that is remaining in the bowl. Cook for 4 hours with the lid on.
8. Remove and serve on a platter, or as a combo meal.

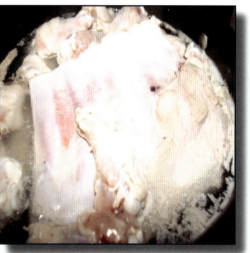

For use with a compact oven follow the above cooking method and cook for 40-50 minutes at 153°C or until golden brown (serves 4-6).

Beef Cobbler

Ingredients

Cobbler ingredients
500g/20oz stewing beef (cubed)
500ml/20fl oz beef stock
(or 2 beef stock cubes and 1 tbsp gravy granules)
2 carrots (peeled and chopped)
1 leek (chopped)
2 sticks of celery (chopped)
150g/6oz mushrooms (sliced)
25g/1oz flour
Salt and pepper
Dumpling ingredients
250g/10oz self raising flour
125g/5oz suet
5fl oz natural yoghurt
Fresh water to mix (if required)
A pinch of dried mixed herbs
Garnish
Fresh parsley
Serves 4-6
(3½ litre slow cooker was used)

Method

1. Mix the beef with the flour in a bowl. Then place cobbler ingredients (beef, carrots, leek, celery, salt and pepper, mushrooms and beef stock) into the Slow Cooker and mix well.
2. Cook on high for 5 hours with the lid on.
3. After 5 hours mix all the dumpling ingredients together in a bowl adding a little water as required to form a stiff dough.
4. Roll out dumpling mix and cut into circles using a pastry cutter. Layer the circles of pastry round the edge of the Slow Cooker and cook for a further 30 minutes on high with the lid on. Season to taste. Garnish with fresh parsley and serve.

With a compact oven halve the amount of ingredients, follow the above cooking method and cook for 2 hours at 153°C adding the dumplings 25 minutes before the end of cooking (serves 2-3).

25

Beef in Black Bean Sauce Q

Ingredients

440g/17¾oz strips of beef
1 red pepper (sliced)
Bunch of spring onions (sliced)
220g jar black bean sauce
4 tbsp water
Garnish
Steamed Pak choi
Serve with rice.
Serves 4-6
(3½ litre slow cooker was used)

Method

1. Place beef inside Crock Pot and set the Slow Cooker onto high.
2. Add the sliced red pepper, sring onion and black bean sauce (add 4 tbsp water to the jar, replace lid and shake, then add this to the Crock Pot)
3. Cook for 5 hours on high with the lid on.
4. Serve on a bed of rice.

For use with a compact follow the above cooking method and cook for 90 minutes at 153°C (serves 4-6).

For use with a compact oven halve the amount of ingredients, follow the above cooking method and cook for 2 hours at 153°C (serves 3).

Chilli Chicken

Ingredients

6 chicken legs
2 tbsp mango chutney
1 tbsp jerk seasoning
½ tsp garlic powder/salt
2 tbsp mayonnaise
¼ tsp garlic paste
½ tsp fresh chilli (finely chopped) optional
1 lime
2 tbsp sweet chilli sauce
75g/3oz suet
50g/2oz bread crumbs
150g/6oz self raising flour
1 lime (halved)

Ingredients for salad dressing
Juice of 1 lime
1 tbsp mango chutney
1 tbsp olive oil
1 tbsp sweet chilli sauce
½ chopped chilli (if desired)
Simply mix and pour onto a green salad.
Serves 4-6
(3½ litre slow cooker was used)

Method

1. Place the chicken, mango chutney, jerk seasoning, garlic powder, mayonnaise, garlic paste, fresh chilli, squeeze of lime, sweet chilli sauce into a bowl and mix together well.
2. Mix the suet, bread crumbs and flour together with a little water, then place in the base of the Crock Pot. Set the Slow Cooker to high.
3. Place the marinated chicken and the squeezed lime on top and cook on high for 5 hours with the lid on.
4. Serve with rice, kidney beans and salad with the mango, chilli and lime dressing. Season to taste.
To make the chicken less fattening you can remove the chicken skin before marinating.

For use with a compact oven halve the amount of ingredients, follow the above cooking method and cook for 90 minutes at 153°C adding the dumplings 25 minutes before the end of cooking (serves 2-3).

Chicken and Sweetcorn Stew with Dumpling Crust

Ingredients

Ingredients for Stew

4 chicken thighs or breast (cubed)
400ml/16fl oz tinned creamed sweetcorn
150g/6oz sweetcorn
300ml/12fl oz chicken stock
1 onion (finely sliced)
¼ tsp garlic paste
1 carrot (peeled and diced)

Ingredients for Corn Dumplings

100ml/4floz creamed sweetcorn
100g/4oz suet
200g/8oz self raising flour
¼ tsp dried herbs
Water to mix

Garnish

Fresh parsley (chopped)

Serve with crusty bread.

Serves 4-6

(5½ litre slow cooker was used)

Method

1. Set the Slow Cooker to high.
2. Add the chicken, creamed sweetcorn, sweetcorn, chicken stock, onion, garlic paste and carrot, mix well and cook for 4 hours with the lid on.
3. Mix together the dumpling ingredients (creamed sweetcorn, suet, flour and dried herbs). Add water slowly until small dumplings can be formed.
4. Place these into the Crock Pot and cook for a further 30 minutes on high with the lid on. Add more water to the stew if necessary.
5. Serve with crusty bread and garnish with the chopped parsley.

Chicken Crumble Q

Ingredients

6 chicken thighs (skinned and boned)
90g/3½oz bread crumbs
340g/13½oz tinned sweetcorn
2 tbsp stuffing mix
Sprigs of thyme
1 tin of condensed chicken & wine soup
(or condensed chicken soup and 2 tbsp
white wine if you prefer)
Serve with steamed vegetables
Serves 4-6
(3½ litre slow cooker was used)

Method

1. Set Slow Cooker to high.
2. Add the condensed soup and sweetcorn to the Crock Pot, then place the chicken thighs on top with a few sprigs of thyme.
3. Mix together the bread crumbs and stuffing in a bowl, then layer this over the chicken and finish with the remaining thyme sprigs.
4. Cook for 5 hours with the lid on.
5. Serve with steamed vegetables.

For use with a compact oven halve the amount of ingredients, follow the above cooking method and cook for 2 hours at 153°C (serves 2-3).

33

Chicken Korma

Ingredients

5 chicken breasts (skinned and cubed)
400ml/16fl oz coconut milk
100g/4oz ground almonds
2 tbsp curry powder
3 tbsp mango chutney
¼ tsp ground chilli powder (optional)
¼ tsp fresh ginger (peeled and chopped)
1 tbsp fresh coriander (chopped)
500ml/20fl oz chicken stock
1 tbsp vegetable oil
1 finely chopped onion
1½ tbsp corn flour (mixed with a little water
 to thicken at end of cooking)
Salt and pepper
Serve with basmati rice and naan bread.
Serves 4-6
(5½ litre slow cooker was used)

Method

1. Set the Slow Cooker to high.
2. Place the coconut milk, mango chutney, ginger, coriander and chicken stock into the Crock Pot and mix well.
3. Using the oil, fry the chicken, onions, chilli powder and curry powder for 4 minutes in a frying pan on a medium heat (to remove the bitterness of the curry powder) then add this mixture to the Crock Pot.
4. Cook for 5 hours with the lid on.
5. Use the cornflour mix to thicken sauce and season to taste.
6. Add the ground almonds then remove and serve with rice and naan bread.

For use with a compact oven halve the amount of ingredients, follow the above cooking method and cook for 90 minutes at 153°C (serves 2-3).

35

Chilli Con Carne

Ingredients

500g/20oz ground beef
¼ tbsp chilli powder
¼ tbsp cayenne powder
1 tin kidney beans in chilli sauce
1 tin of tomatoes
2 tbsp tomato puree
4 tbsp tomato ketchup
1 onion (finely chopped)
¼ tbsp paprika
1 carrot (peeled and diced)
100g/4oz mushrooms (sliced)
1 tbsp plain flour
1 clove of garlic (finely chopped)
3 tomatoes (quartered)
½ litre/20fl oz beef stock
Serve with rice, cheese and tortilla chips.
Serves 4-6
(6½ litre slow cooker was used)

Method

1. Set the Slow Cooker to high and add the chilli powder, cayenne powder, kidney beans, tinned tomatoes, tomato puree, tomato ketchup, onion, paprika, carrot, mushrooms, garlic and fresh tomatoes. Then mix in the flour and stir in the beef stock.
2. In a large pan, fry the mince until browned, draining off fat as necessary, then add to the Crock pot.
3. Cook on high for 5 hours with lid on.
4. Serve with rice, cheese and tortilla chips.

For use with a compact oven halve the amount of ingredients, follow the above cooking method cook for 2 hours at 153°C (serves 2-3).

37

Cod Parcels

Ingredients

2 cod portions
50g/2oz prawns
25g/1oz butter
¼ tsp ginger (peeled and finely chopped)
2 spring onions (sliced)
2 tsp light soy sauce
200g/8oz long grain rice
1 carrot (peeled and chopped)
1 spring onion (sliced)
1 courgette (diced)
1 litre/40fl oz vegetable stock
1 yellow pepper (diced)
1 tomato (diced)
1 tbsp light soy sauce
Serve with pak choi, salad and dressing.
Serves 2
(3½ litre slow cooker was used)

Method

1. Place the rice, carrot, one spring onion sliced, courgette, vegetable stock, yellow pepper, tomato and light soy sauce into the Crock Pot on high, mix well and replace lid.
2. Place a cod portion, butter, ginger, prawns, one spring onion and soy sauce onto a square of tin foil and wrap to secure. Repeat with other portion.
3. The parcels need to be supported, (I use metal food rings for this) placed in the base of the Slow Cooker on top of the rice mixture. Cook for 4 hours with the lid on.

For use with a compact oven follow the above cooking method and cook for 50 minutes at 153°C (serves 2).

Duck Cassoulet

Ingredients
4 duck legs
1 onion (sliced)
4 celery sticks (chopped)
2 garlic cloves (finely chopped)
150g/6oz spicy Toulouse sausage
(or your favourite sausage)
Salt and pepper
2 bay leaves
2 tins of tomatoes
¼ litre/10fl oz chicken stock
100g/4oz bread crumbs to thicken
1 carrot (peeled and chopped)
1 tin of haricot beans (drained)
1 tin 400g/16oz cannellini beans (drained)
Serve with sauté potatoes and
steamed vegetables.
Serves 4-6
(6½ litre slow cooker was used)

Method

1. Place the duck legs, onions, celery, garlic, sausage, bay leaves, salt and pepper, tomatoes, chicken stock, carrot, haricot and cannellini beans (leaving out the bread crumbs at this stage) into Crock Pot. Mix well then cook on high for 5½ hours with lid on.
2. After this time, add the bread crumbs and cook for a further 30 minutes with lid on.
3. Season to taste.

For use with the compact oven halve the amount of the ingredients, and don't use any haricot beans, follow the above cooking method and cook for 2 hours at 153°C (serves 2-3).

41

Duck with Hoisin Sauce and Noodles

Ingredients

1 duck crown or 2 duck breasts
2 large or 4 small spring onions
(sliced diagonally)
3 carrots (sliced diagonally)
1 fennel bulb
3 tbsp hoisin sauce
1 tbsp soy sauce
2 star anise
1 onion (peeled and halved)
pak choi
Chicken flavour noodles (includes sachet)
(if using normal noodles,
1 x chicken stock cube is required)
Serve with chilli sauce
Serves 4-6
(6½ litre slow cooker was used)

Method

1. Set the Slow Cooker to high.
2. Place 4 tbsp water in Crock Pot with the chopped spring onions, carrots and the whole fennel bulb. Place lid on.
3. Score the duck crown across the skin in a crisscross pattern. In a pan of boiling water, place duck crown, star anise, soy sauce, onion, halve of the hoisin sauce and *either* the sachet of chicken flavouring from the noodles *or* the chicken stock cube. Boil for 30 minutes and skim off excess fat and froth.
4. Once boiled add the crown and broth to the Crock Pot. Cover the crown with the remaining hoisin sauce, cook on high for 4 hours with the lid on.
5. Cook the noodles and pak choi on your stove.
6. Place the duck on a bed of the noodles and pak choi along with the broth, fennel, carrots and spring onions. Serve with chilli sauce.

For use with a compact oven follow the above cooking method and cook for 90 minutes at 153°C (serves 2-3).

Gammon Joint with Peaches

Ingredients

1 gammon joint
1 tin of peaches in syrup
1 clove of garlic (finely chopped)
1 onion (finely chopped)
Salt and pepper to taste
1 chicken stock cube
25ml/1fl oz boiling water
1 tbsp cider vinegar
¼ tsp dried mixed herbs
**Serve with mashed potatoes
and steamed vegetables
Serves 4-6
(3½ litre slow cooker was used)**

Method

1. Boil gammon joint for 30 minutes in a pan of boiling water to remove some of the salt.
2. Set the Slow Cooker to high.
3. Place the gammon joint with the tin of peaches inside the Crock Pot.
4. Break up chicken stock cube and mix with the 1fl oz boiling water add to gammon joint together with garlic, onions, cider vinegar and mixed herbs then mix together well and season.
5. Cook for 5 hours with the lid on.
6. Remove and serve with mashed potatoes and steamed vegetables.

For use with a compact oven follow the above cooking method and cook for 2 hours at 153°C (serves 4-6).

45

Haggis Q

Ingredients

½ swede (peeled and halved)
2 carrots (peeled)
2 large potatoes
1 haggis
1 litre/40fl oz water
3 sprigs rosemary
3 tbsp gravy granules
Serves 4
(3½ litre slow cooker was used)
Butter & season to taste.

Method

1. Set Slow Cooker to high
2. Place the haggis, potatoes, swede, carrots, rosemary and water into the Crock Pot.
3. Cook for 4 hours with the lid on.
4. After cooking remove the haggis, potatoes, carrots, swede and rosemary.
5. Mash the potatoes and vegetables seasoning and adding butter to taste.
6. Add the gravy granules to the left over liquid, stirring until it thickens.
7. Serve over the haggis and with mashed vegetables.
   Butter and season to taste.

For use with a compact oven follow the above cooking method and cook for 2½ hours at 153°C (serves 4).

Lamb Chops with a Mint and Redcurrant Gravy

Ingredients

3 lamb chops
1 onion (roughly chopped)
2 tbsp chicken stock
8 large new potatoes
½ swede (peeled)
2 tbsp redcurrant jelly
3 tsp mint sauce
2 tbsp gravy granules
Serves 3
(3½ litre slow cooker was used)

Method

1. Set the Slow Cooker to high.
2. Place the onions and chicken stock inside Crock Pot.
3. Mix together the mint sauce and red currant jelly in a bowl.
4. Place lamb chops into Crock pot and then drizzle with the mint sauce and redcurrant jelly.
5. Arrange the potatoes and swede around the chops.
6. Cook for 4 hours with the lid on and serve.
7. Remove the lamb chops, potatoes and vegetables then add gravy granules, stir, then add boiling water to your desired consistency.

For use with a compact oven cut the potatoes in halve and swede into quarters, then follow the above cooking method and cook for 2 hours at 153°C or until the potatoes soften (serves 3).

49

Lamb Joint

Ingredients

1 lamb joint (leg)
2 sprigs rosemary
2 garlic cloves (sliced)
9 large new potatoes
4 whole carrots (peeled)
2 celery sticks (chopped)
1 onion (finely chopped)
1 parsnip (peeled)
250ml/10fl oz beef stock
2 tbsp gravy granules
Serves 2-4
(6½ litre slow cooker was used)

Method

1. Set the Slow Cooker to high.
2. Stud/pierce the lamb joint with the rosemary and garlic.
3. Place the celery and onion in the base of the Crock Pot, then place the lamb joint on top.
4. Place the potatoes, carrots and parsnip around the joint.
5. Pour the beef stock into the Crock Pot and season.
6. Cook for 5 to 6 hours with the lid on.
7. Remove lamb joint, potatoes and vegetables, place them on a platter then cover with tin foil and a tea towel to allow the meat to rest.
8. To make gravy with the meat juice residue, simply add the gravy granules and 80ml/3¼fl oz boiling water to the Crock Pot, mix well and allow to cook out on high for 10 minutes with the lid on.
9. Serve gravy over the lamb, potatoes and vegetables.

For use with a compact oven, cut the potatoes in halve then follow the above cooking method and cook for 2 hours at 153°C (serves 2-4).

Lamb Kleftiko

Ingredients

400g/16oz shoulder of lamb (cubed)
2 cloves garlic (finely chopped)
½ tsp olive oil
2 onions (sliced)
2 tbsp plain flour
125ml/5fl oz chicken stock
125ml/5fl oz white wine
2 tbsp cider vinegar
1 tbsp honey
1 sprig rosemary
½ lemon
2 tbsp parsley
Salt and pepper
**Serve with mashed/roast potatoes
or rice and steamed vegetables.
Serves 4-6
(5½ litre slow cooker was used)**

Method

1. Place lamb into a bowl and squeeze the juice of the lemon over it. Allow this to marinate for ten minutes prior to cooking.
2. Fry off the lamb in a little oil for 4 minutes in a hot frying pan to brown slightly.

3. Set the Slow Cooker to high, place the lamb, garlic, oil, onions, chicken stock, wine, vinegar, honey, rosemary and parsley into the Slow Cooker, leaving the flour until the end, then sprinkle it over the other ingredients and mix well.
4. Cook for five hours with the lid on.
5. Remove and serve with potatoes, rice and steamed vegetables. Season to taste.

**For use with a compact oven follow the above cooking method
and cook for 2½ hours at 153°C (serves 4-6).**

Lamb Rogan Josh Q

Ingredients
500g/20oz lamb chops
425g/17oz jar Rogan Josh sauce
3 tomatoes
5 new potatoes (halved)
Serve on a bed of rice.
Serves 4-6
(3½ litre slow cooker was used)

Method
1. Set the Slow Cooker to high.
2. Chop up one tomato and place into the Crock Pot. Then place the lamb on top.
3. Quarter the remaining tomatoes and layer on top of the lamb, then add the halved potatoes.
4. Add the lamb Rogan Josh sauce (add 4 tbsp water to the jar once emptied, replace lid and shake, add this to the Crock Pot).
5. Cook for 5 hours on high with the lid on.
   Serve on a bed of rice.

For use with a compact oven follow the above cooking method and cook for 2 hours at 153°C (serves 4-6).

Lamb Shank

Ingredients

2 lamb shanks
1 onion (sliced)
125ml/5 fl oz red wine
100g/4oz mushrooms (sliced)
 2 tbsp redcurrant jelly
125ml/5 fl oz gravy granules
1 sprig rosemary
Serve with mashed potato
and vegetables.
Serves 2
(6½ litre slow cooker was used)

Method

1. Place ingredients, lamb, onion, red wine, mushrooms, redcurrant jelly, rosemary into Crock Pot.
2. Mix ½ pint of boiling water with the gravy granules stir and add to the Crock Pot, season and cook on high for 6 hours with lid on.
3. Remove and serve on bed of mashed potatoes and vegetables.

For use with a compact oven follow the above cooking method and cook for 3 hours at 153°C (serves 2).

Liver with Bacon

Ingredients

4 rashers of back bacon
300g/12oz pig's liver
250ml/10fl oz gravy
(you can use gravy granules)
1 onion (finely chopped)
125ml/5fl oz beef stock
1 tbsp parsley
2 tbsp flour
¼ tsp dried mixed herbs
Salt and pepper to taste.
**Serve with mashed potatoes
and vegetables.
Serves 4-6
(3½ litre slow cooker was used)**

Method

1. Cut the liver into small slices and dip in seasoned flour, (flour seasoned with salt and pepper) shake off excess and place in Crock Pot and set Slow Cooker to high, then add bacon, gravy, onions, parsley, beef stock and mixed herbs.
2. Cook on high for 5 hours with lid on.
3. Remove and serve with mashed potatoes and vegetables.

For use with a compact oven follow the above cooking method and cook for 2 hours at 153°C (serves 4-6).

Meat Balls in a Spicy Sauce

Ingredients

500g/20oz minced beef
1 onion (finely chopped)
3 tbsp of plain flour
1 egg
ground black pepper
¼ tsp garlic salt/granules

Sauce Ingredients

1 tsp dried chilli powder
½ tsp garlic salt/granules
4 tbsp tomato sauce
2 tbsp tomato puree
1 onion (finely chopped)
1 garlic clove (finely chopped)
¼ tsp mixed dried herbs
2 tins of chopped tomatoes
4 fresh tomatoes (quartered)

Serve with spaghetti and parmesan.
Serves 4-6
(5½ litre slow cooker was used)

Method

1. Set the Slow Cooker to high.
2. Place the chilli powder, garlic, garlic salt, tomato sauce, tomato purée, onions, mixed herbs, chopped tomatoes and fresh quartered tomatoes into the Crock Pot and mix well.
3. Place the mince, black pepper, egg, garlic salt and onion in a large bowl, mix these together then slowly begin to add the flour, mixing all the time.
4. Once all the flour has been added, roll the mixture into balls (just smaller than a ping pong ball) using a little extra flour to dust hands if necessary.
5. Add the balls to the Crock Pot and cook for 5 hours with the lid on.
6. Remove season and serve with spaghetti and parmesan.
   If you prefer non spicy food, leave out the chilli powder.

For use in a compact oven halve the amount of ingredients, follow the above cooking method and cook for 2 hours at 153°C (serves 2-3).

61

Mediterranean Pork Q

Ingredients

 4 pork shoulder steaks
(200g/8oz approximately each)
100g/4oz olives and feta
1 can chopped tomatoes
10 new potatoes (halved)
1 can condensed tomato soup
Serve with rice.
Serves 2-4
(3½ litre slow cooker was used)

Method

1. Set the Slow Cooker to high.
2. Pour the chopped tomatoes in the base
   of the Crock Pot and then place the pork
   steaks on top.
3. Cover the pork with the tomato soup, then add the olive feta mix and
   layer the new potatoes over the top.
4. Cook for 5 hours with the lid on.

For use with a compact oven halve the amount of ingredients,
follow the above cooking method and cook for 2 hours at 153°C
(serves 2).

Moroccan Stew

Ingredients

300g/12oz lamb shoulder (cubed)
1 large onion (sliced)
1 garlic clove (finely chopped)
½ tsp ground cumin
¼ tsp ground coriander
¼ tsp ground paprika
½ tsp chopped parsley
½ lemon (juiced), 1 tsp zest
2 tbsp honey
2 tinned tomatoes
125ml/5fl oz chicken stock
1 sweet potato (peeled and diced)
1 400g/16oz tin chickpeas (drained)
50g/2oz sultanas
3 tbsp flour
1 large or 2 medium potatoes (chopped)
Serve with cous cous, sour cream mixed with mint jelly.
Serves 4-6
(3½ litre slow cooker was used)

Method

1. Marinate the lamb in a bowl with the lemon juice for 10 minutes prior to cooking.
2. Set the Slow Cooker to high. Place the onion, garlic, cumin, coriander, paprika, parsley, honey, tomatoes, chicken stock, sweet potato, flour, chickpeas, sultanas, and potatoes into the Crock Pot and mix well.
3. Add the lamb and remaining lemon juice then cook for 5 hours with the lid on, stirring every 2 hours.
4. Remove season to taste and serve with regular cous cous or large cous cous and sour cream mixed with mint jelly.

For use with a compact oven halve the amount of ingredients, follow the above cooking method and cook for 2 hours at 153°C (serves 2-3).

Mushroom Chicken Q

Ingredients

4 chicken breasts (skinned)
1 can condensed mushroom soup (295g)
5 large mushrooms (sliced)
8 large new potatoes (halved)
Fresh or dried tarragon (dried is better)
Serves 4
(3½ litre slow cooker was used)

Method

1. Set the Slow Cooker to high.
2. Place half the fresh mushrooms in the base of the Slow Cooker.
3. Place the chicken on top of the mushroom layer and then add the remaining sliced mushrooms.
4. Layer the chopped potatoes over the chicken and mushrooms and pour the whole can of soup over the top. Roughly chop the tarragon and sprinkle over.
5. Cook for 5 hours on high with the lid on.

For use with a compact oven follow the above cooking method and cook for 2 hours at 153°C (serves 4).

67

Pork and Pineapple Q

Ingredients

4 pork slices/steaks
75g sun dried tomatoes
225g tin pineapple rings in syrup
100g tomato sauce
2 tbsp vinegar
1 tbsp cornflour to thicken if necessary
Serve with rice and steamed pak choi.
Serves 4
(5½ litre slow cooker was used)

Method

1. Set the Slow Cooker to high.
2. Cut excess fat off the pork slices/steaks and add the trimmed pork to Crock Pot. Place pineapple on top (with syrup), then tomatoes, vinegar and tomato sauce. Cook for 5 hours on high with lid on.
3. To thicken the sauce, mix the cornflour with a little cold water and add to the Crock Pot, stir well.
4. Serve with rice.

For use with a compact oven follow the above cooking method and cook for 2 hours at 153°C (serves 4).

Prawn Biriani

Ingredients

200g/8oz large shelled prawns
2 tbsp curry powder
1 tin of tomatoes
1 sweet potato (peeled and diced)
1 carrot (peeled and diced)
300g/12oz mushrooms (sliced)
300g/12oz basmati rice
50g/2oz French beans
1 litre/40fl oz chicken or vegetable stock
2 tbsp sweet chilli sauce
Serve with poppadoms and mango chutney.
Serves 4-6
(3½ litre slow cooker was used)

Method

1. Set the Slow Cooker to high.
2. Place all the ingredients (prawns, curry powder, tomatoes, sweet potatoes, carrots, mushrooms, basmati rice, French beans, stock and sweet chilli sauce) into the Crock Pot.
3. Mix well and cook for 3-4 hours (depending on the power and size of your Slow Cooker) with the lid on.
4. For best results serve immediately with poppadoms and mango chutney.

For use with a compact oven, halve the amount of ingredients, follow the above cooking method and cook for 90 minutes at 153°C (serves 2-3).

71

Roast Beef with Suet Crust

Ingredients

1 kg/2.2lbs beef joint
1 onion (sliced)
100g/4oz suet
200g/8oz self-raising flour
Salt and pepper
1-2 tbsps gravy granules
1 tbsp oil
6 large new potatoes
3 carrots (peeled)
1 parsnip (peeled)

Serves 4-6
(5½ litre slow cooker was used)

Method

1. Seal the beef joint in a hot frying pan.
2. Set the Slow Cooker to high and add the onion and oil. Place the beef joint into Slow Cooker and season.
3. Place carrots, parsnip and potatoes around the beef and cook for 5 hours on high, with lid on.
4. Mix the flour and suet with a little cold water to form suet pastry and place this around the edge of the joint.
5. Cook for a further 40 minutes.
6. Remove the beef, vegetables and suet crust. Add some gravy granules to the juices left inside the Crock Pot, mix together, add boiling water (amount depending on preferred consistency.) Cook on high for 5 minutes with lid on to make a delicious gravy.

For use with a compact oven halve the amount of ingredients, follow the above cooking method and cook 2 1/2 hours for well done or to your preference at 153°C, adding the suet crust 25 minutes before the end of cooking (serves 2-3).

73

Roast Chicken Q

Ingredients

1 medium chicken
10 pigs in blankets
 (mini sausages wrapped in bacon)
1 small swede (peeled & quartered)
2 parsnips (peeled & halved)
2 carrots (peeled & halved)
1 leek (sliced)
1 sweet potato (peeled & quartered)
125ml water
2 tbsp gravy granules
10 new potatoes
¼ tsp mixed herbs
Serve with green vegetables
Serves 4-6
(6½ litre slow cooker was used)

Method

1. Set the Slow Cooker to high.
2. Place leek in base of Crock Pot, together with chicken and surround with swede, carrots, potatoes, parsnips and sweet potato. Pour on water.
3. Put pigs in blankets around the chicken and sprinkle with the mixed herbs.
4. Cook for 5 hours on high.
5. Place all ingredients onto a serving platter, leaving the juice in the Crock Pot. Add 75ml boiling water and gravy granules and mix well. Pour over chicken.
6. Serve with fresh green vegetables .

For use with a compact oven use a small chicken, halve the amount of the rest of the ingredients, follow the above cooking method and cook for 2 hours at 153°C or until cooked (serves 2-3). 75

Salmon Parcels

Ingredients

2 salmon portions
25g/1oz butter (salted)
1 x lemon (cut into 4)
Salt
Pepper
8 large new potatoes
Salsa
1 x tomato (diced)
½ mango (diced)
½ red onion (finely chopped)
¼ red chilli (optional)
1 tbsp coriander (chopped)
½ tbsp mango chutney
½ tbsp sweet chilli sauce
Serve with French bean salad
and tomato, mango salsa.
Serves 2
(3½ litre slow cooker was used)

Method

1. Place one salmon, ½ butter and ½ lemon together, season and wrap in tin foil.
2. Repeat for other portion.
3. Set the Slow Cooker to high.
4. Add salmon parcels to the Crock Pot with 2 cups of boiled water and put new potatoes around the outside.
5. Cook for 2 hours (or until cooked) with lid on. Season to taste.
6. Combine the salsa ingredients and leave to marinate in the fridge until salmon is ready to serve.
   Serve with french bean salad and tomato, mango salsa.

For use with a compact oven cut the potatoes into quarters and halve the amount of water then follow the above cooking method and cook for 1 hour and 10 minutes at 153°C (serves 2).

Slow Roasted Pork Loin with BBQ Sauce

Ingredients

Shoulder of pork (weight 1kg approx)
2 tbsp cider vinegar
1 tbsp soft, dark brown sugar
2 tbsp honey
5 tbsp BBQ sauce
4 tbsp tomato sauce
1 tbsp tomato puree
1½ tsp garlic paste
1 tbsp soy sauce
1 onion (sliced)

Serve with mashed potatoes and corn on the cob.
Serves 4-6
(6½ litre slow cooker was used)

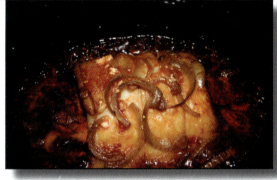

Method

1. Set the Slow Cooker to high and place pork joint and onions in the Crock Pot.
2. Place the cider vinegar, sugar, honey, BBQ sauce, tomato sauce, tomato purée, garlic paste, soy sauce in a bowl and mix well.
3. Pour this mixture over the pork and onions.
4. Cook for 6 hours with the lid on. At the end of cooking time, drain off fat, the gravy can be thickened with cornflour, if desired, by mixing 2 tsp cornflour with 2 tbsp of cold water and adding to the hot gravy.
5. Remove and serve with mashed potatoes and corn on the cob.

For use with a compact oven follow the above cooking method and cook for 3 hours at 153°C or until the juices run clear (serves 4-6).

Sauce Bolognese

Ingredients

300g/12oz minced beef
100ml/4fl oz of white or red wine
3 rashers of bacon (chopped) or pancetta
1 onion (finely chopped)
2 x tins tomatoes
2 tbsp tomato puree
¼ tsp mixed dried herbs
8 medium mushrooms (sliced)
1 tbsp sugar
6 fresh basil leaves
1 bay leaf
2 cloves of garlic (finely chopped)
2 tbsp of olive oil
Garnish
chopped parsley and grated parmesan.
Serve with spaghetti.
Serves 4-6
(3½ litre slow cooker was used)

Method

1. Set Slow Cooker to high and add the wine, bacon, onion, both tins of tomatoes, tomato puree, mixed herbs, mushrooms, basil leaves, sugar, bay leaf, garlic and olive oil, mix well and put the lid on.
2. Fry the minced beef in a pan until brown, drain off excess fat if necessary, add to Crock Pot and mix well.
3. Season and cook for 5 hours on high with the lid on, stirring occasionally.
4. Serve with spaghetti and garnish with freshly grated parmesan and chopped parsley.

For use with a compact oven halve the amount of tinned tomatoes then follow the above cooking method and cook for 2 hours at 153°C (serves 4-5).

Steak and Ale Pudding

Ingredients

250g/10oz stewing beef (cubed)
100mls / 6fl oz ale
75ml beef gravy
1 onion (chopped)
Pinch of salt and pepper
75g/3oz mushrooms (sliced)
(for a nice flavour use chestnut mushrooms)
¼ tsp dried mixed herbs
½ tbsp flour

Suet pastry ingredients
200g/8oz suet
400g/16oz self-raising flour
¼ tsp mixed dried herbs

Serve with mash potatoes &
steamed vegetables.
Serves 4-6
(3½ litre slow cooker was used)

Method

1. Set Slow Cooker to high, fill with 2 litres of boiling water, place lid on.
2. Mix suet, adding self-raising flour, salt, pepper and mixed herbs.
3. Add a little water to the mix until it forms a dough, knead well and roll out on to a board using a little flour to prevent sticking.
4. Line a 1 litre pudding basin with pastry (keeping enough to form a lid.)
5. Place the stewing beef, ale, gravy, onion, mushrooms, mixed herbs, flour, salt and pepper into a large bowl and mix together well.
6. Place this mix into the lined pudding basin and cover with suet lid.
7. Cover the pudding basin with cling film ensuring it covers down the sides,then cover with tin foil.
8. Place carefully into the Slow Cooker, cook for 7 hours with the lid on.
9. Remove and serve with mashed potatoes and steamed vegetables.

For use with a compact oven follow the above cooking method with 1 litre pudding basin, replace the clingfilm with greaseproof paper and cook for 4 hours in half the amount of cooking water at 153°C topping up the cooking water if necessary (serves 4-6).

83

Stuffed Chicken Thighs

Ingredients

6 boneless skinless chicken thighs
50g/2oz sage & onion stuffing mix
6 rashers of unsmoked back bacon
1 tbsp redcurrant jelly
50g/2oz sausage meat (or 1 sausage skinned)
3 whole carrots
12 new potatoes
1 onion (chopped)
200ml/8fl oz chicken stock
Serve with steamed French green beans.
Serves 4-6
(3½ litre slow cooker was used)

Method

1. Add the stuffing to the bowl, pour over boiling water to make a firm mix.
2. Then mix the stuffing with the sausage meat and redcurrant jelly.
3. Spread out the chicken thighs and place the stuffing mix in each thigh, then wrap the thigh with bacon.
4. Place onion in the bottom of the Crock Pot, add the stuffed chicken thighs, then place the new potatoes and whole peeled carrots on top.
5. Pour in the chicken stock, cook for 5 hours on high with the lid on.
6. Remove meat and vegetables. Use remaining juices to make gravy by mixing with some gravy granules and adding more boiling water if required.

For use with a compact oven halve the amount of ingredients, follow the above cooking method and cook for 2 hours at 153°C (serves 2-3).

85

Sweet Chilli Pork Q

Ingredients

500g cubed pork
1 red pepper (sliced)
1 courgette (sliced)
295g tin condensed tomato soup
75ml sweet chilli sauce
Serve with noodles or rice.
Serves 4-6
(1½ litre slow cooker was used)

Method

1. Set the Slow Cooker to high.
2. Pour the soup into the Crock Pot and place the pork on top.
3. Add the courgette, red pepper and sweet chilli sauce.
4. Cook for 4 hours with the lid on.
5. Serve with noodles or rice.

For use with a compact oven follow the above cooking method and cook for 2 hours at 153°C (serves 4-6).

87

Tomato and Seafood Linguine

Ingredients

300g/12oz seafood mix
6 fresh tomatoes (quartered)
2 tbsp tomato puree
½ tbsp olive oil
½ tsp garlic paste
1 onion (finely chopped)
1 tbsp sweet chilli sauce
2 x tins chopped tomatoes
½ tsp dried mixed herbs

Garnish

Basil

Serve with cooked linguine pasta, parmesan and chopped parsley.
Serves 6-8
(1½ litre slow cooker was used.)

Method

1. Set the Slow Cooker to high.
2. Place fresh tomatoes, tomato puree, olive oil, garlic paste, onion, sweet chilli sauce, tins of tomatoes and mixed herbs into Crock pot. Cook for 4 hours with the lid on.
3. After 4 hours add the seafood mix.
4. Cook on high for a further 30 minutes.
5. Six minutes before serving cook linguine pasta in boiling salt water, remove and serve with pasta, parmesan and chopped parsley. Garnish with basil and season to taste.

For use with a compact oven follow the above cooking method and cook for 90 minutes then add the cooked seafood and cook for a further 15 minutes at 153°C (serves 6-8).

Baked Cheesecake

Ingredients

200g/8oz digestive biscuits (crushed)
75g/3oz brown sugar
75g/3oz butter (melted)

Ingredients for Topping

500g/20oz full fat cream cheese
150g/6oz caster sugar
3 whole eggs
1 egg yolk
2 lemons (juice and zest)
2 tbsp candied peel/mix peel
200g lemon curd

Serve with grapefruit, orange, lime segments or strawberries.
Serves 4-6
(6½ litre slow cooker was used.)

Method

1. Carefully add 1 litre/40 fl oz of boiling water into Crock Pot and set Slow Cooker to high.
2. Place the biscuits, brown sugar and butter into a bowl and mix, then place the mixture in an oven proof dish, 8 to 9 inches across or a 2lb loaf tin if that fits better. Press down firmly to flatten.
3. Mix the cream cheese, sugar, eggs, egg yolk, lemon and candied peel in a bowl and add to oven dish/loaf tin.
4. Cover with cling film and then tin foil, fold down the sides to secure.
5. Place this into the Crock Pot ensuring the water only reaches halfway up the side of the bowl. Add or remove water as necessary.
6. Cook for 4 hours with the lid on. After cooking time, remove and allow to cool for 1 hour then cover with lemon curd. Chill in fridge and serve.

For use with a compact oven use two thirds of the ingredients follow the above cooking method but use a 1½ litre, (20cm diameter oven dish), replace the clingfilm with greaseproof paper and cook in halve the amount of water for 90 minutes at 153°C topping up the cooking water if neccesary (serves 4-5).

91

Banoffee Pie

Ingredients

2 bananas (sliced)
2 tins sweetened condensed milk
(370g each)
1 packet of oat biscuits
1 chocolate flake
50g/2oz butter (melted)
1 pint double cream (whipped)
Serves 4-6
(5½ litre slow cooker was used.)

Method

1. Add freshly boiled water to the Crock Pot, set the Slow Cooker to high and place the tins of condensed milk in the Crock pot. Leave for 4 to 5 hours with the lid on. **Never open tin whilst hot!.**
2. Mix the oat biscuits in a food processor with the butter and place in the base of a serving dish approximately 6-8 inch across. Pat the mixture down and leave to cool in the fridge.
3. Once the sweetened condensed milk has been cooked for 4-5 hours, remove tins and allow to cool in cold water, until the tins are cold, then open carefully.
4. Spoon the cooked milk onto the biscuit base (saving some back for decoration) add the sliced bananas and allow pie to cool in the fridge.
5. Once cool, cover with scoops of whipped double cream. Crumble the flake all over the pie together with the remaining condensed milk and serve.

For use in a compact oven add 1ltr of boiling water to the oven dish, place the tins in the water, cover with tin foil and cook for 2 hours at 153°C allow the tins to cool in the oven for 30 minutes, transfer to cold water for further cooling then follow the method above (serves 4-6).

Boiled Fruit Cake

Ingredients

12oz/300g mixed fruit
4oz/100g dark brown soft sugar
4oz/100g soft butter or margarine
¼pt/10fl oz water
4oz/100g glacé cherries
2 eggs
8oz/200g self-raising flour
½ tsp mixed spice
Brown sugar for dusting cake at end
of cooking
Serves 4-6
(6½ litre slow cooker was used.)

Method

1. Place the mixed fruit, glacé cherries, mixed spice, butter, brown sugar and water into a pan. Bring to the boil for 5 minutes.
2. Allow to cool, slowly add the eggs then the flour, ensuring that you mix them well. Once mixed pour into a 2 lb grease proof lined cake or loaf tin (that will fit inside your Slow Cooker).
3. Set the Slow Cooker to high and add 1 litre of freshly boiled water. Cover the cake tin with cling film then tin foil and place in Crock Pot.
4. Cook for 5 to 6 hours on high with lid on, then take out and allow to cool.
5. Dust with brown sugar and serve with a nice cup of tea.

For use with a compact oven use two thirds of the ingredients, follow the above cooking method but use a 1½ litre (20cm diameter oven dish), replace the clingfilm with greaseproof paper and cook in halve the amount of water for 2 hours at 153°C topping up the cooking water if necessary (serves 4-5).

95

Bread and Butter Pudding

Ingredients
25 slices of white bread
75g/3oz butter
125g/5oz sultanas
150g6oz brown caster sugar
75g/3oz dried apricots (chopped)
1 orange zest
100ml/4fl oz double cream
800ml/32fl oz whole milk
5 eggs
¼ grated nutmeg
3 tbsp orange liqueur (optional)
1 tbsp corn flour (mixed with milk
or water to form a paste)
Serves 6-8
(6½ litre slow cooker was used.)

Method

1. Set the Slow Cooker to high and add 6 tbsp of milk.
2. Lightly butter the bread. Place layers of bread, sultanas, dried apricots and orange zest into the Crock Pot, leaving some back for the top of the pudding, (cut the bread to fit as necessary).
3. Mix the cream, milk, eggs, 5oz brown sugar and the corn flour paste. Pass this mixture through a sieve and then mix in the nutmeg.
4. Pour this mixture over the bread layers in the Crock Pot and then cover with the rest of the brown sugar, sultanas and fruit.
5. Cook for 3½ hours with the lid on or until cooked.
6. Remove and serve each portion with some cream or custard.

For use in a compact oven use a third of the ingredients, and place in a 2ltr dish, and follow the above cooking method and cook for 35-40 minutes at 153°C (serves 4-6).

For use in a compact oven follow the cooking method but use a 1½ litre (20cm diameter) oven dish, replace the cling film with greaseproof paper and cook in halve the amount of water for 2½ hours at 153°C topping up the cooking water if necessary (serves 4-6).

Carrot Cake

Ingredients

Cake Ingredients

200g/8oz self raising flour

1 tsp baking powder

1 tsp mixed spice

½ tsp nutmeg

125g/5oz butter/margarine (room temp)

125g/5oz soft brown sugar

2 eggs (lightly beaten)

2 carrots (peeled and grated)

125g/5oz mixed fruit

50g/2oz walnuts, leaving some for decoration

2 tbsp milk

75g/3oz pineapple (finely chopped)

Topping Ingredients

1 orange (zest)

1 tsp orange juice

100g/4oz icing sugar

150g/6oz cream cheese

25g/1oz butter

Serves 4-6

(6½ litre slow cooker was used.)

Method

1. Mix the butter and brown sugar until fluffy, slowly beat in the eggs. Add flour, baking powder, nutmeg and mixed spice, mix well and add the mixed fruit and grated carrots. Mix together with some of the walnuts and pineapple. (Can use a food mixer for this).

2. Set the Slow Cooker to high and add ½ litre boiling water to the Crock Pot. Place the cake mixture into a greased 2lb loaf tin, cover the loaf tin with cling film, then tin foil and carefully place inside Slow Cooker.

3. Cook for 5 to 6 hours with the lid on or until cooked. After cooking time, take out the cake and allow to cool on a baking rack. Place the cream cheese, butter, icing sugar, orange zest and 1 tsp of the orange juice in a bowl and mix well.

4. Cover the cake with the topping and arrange walnuts on top. Serve with a nice cup of tea or coffee.

99

Cheats Fruit Crumble Q

Ingredients

4 tbsp maple syrup
400g/16oz apples
 (peeled cored and cubed)
200g/8oz blackberries
 (fresh or frozen)
Crumble Ingredients
2 slices bread
5 oat biscuits
200g/8oz cake (e.g. lemon)
Serve with fresh cream
Serves 4-6
(5½ litre slow cooker was used.)

Method

1. Set the Slow Cooker to high.
2. Mix together the apple, berries and maple syrup then place into the Crock Pot with lid on, on high for 3 hours.
3. Place the bread, biscuits and cake in a bowl, in a food processor until the mixture resembles bread crumbs. Sprinkle this mixture over the fruit to create a top layer, and serve (the crumble mix requires no cooking).

For use in a compact oven follow the above cooking method and cook for 50 minutes at 153°C until fruit is soft (serves 4-6).

For use in a compact oven follow the cooking method and cook in halve the amount of water for 3½ hours at 153°C topping up the cooking water if necessary (serves 4-6).

Christmas Pudding

Ingredients

1 eating apple (peeled, cored & grated)
100g/4oz raisins
175g/7oz luxury mixed fruit (with cherries, dried pineapple, candied peel)
75g/3oz dark candied cherries
75ml/3fl oz brandy/cherry brandy or rum
(I use half cherry brandy, half rum)
1 carrot (grated)
Juice and zest of 1 orange
2 eggs
100g/4oz plain flour
62g/2½oz suet
37g/1½ tbsp black treacle
100g/4oz dark muscovado sugar
75g/3oz fresh breadcrumbs
¼ tsp nutmeg
¼ tsp mixed spice
1oz pecan nuts (optional)
1oz ground almonds (optional)
Serves 4-6
(5½ litre slow cooker was used.)

Method

1. Set Slow Cooker to high and carefully pour in 2 pints of boiling water.
2. Place the apple, raisins, mixed fruit, candied cherries, brandy/rum, carrot, orange, eggs, flour, suet, treacle, sugar, breadcrumbs, nutmeg, mixed spice, pecans, ground almonds, in a bowl and mix together.
3. Place the mixed ingredients in a greased 2 pint pudding basin.
4. Cover with a circle of grease proof paper then tin foil.
5. Lower the basin into Crock Pot by making a lifting strap out of tin foil, ensuring that the hot water comes halfway up the pudding basin.
6. Cook for 7 hours with the lid on. Allow to cool in a cool place to keep the pudding ready for the big day. You can add more brandy if required by putting a tablespoon of brandy or rum under the grease proof paper allowing it to soak in slowly, (amount depends on your taste).
7. Serve hot with brandy butter or clotted/double cream.

103

For use in a compact oven use the cooking method, but do not cover the ramekins and cook for 25-30 minutes at 153°C (serves 4).

Crème Caramel

Ingredients

Caramel Ingredient
4 tbsp golden syrup
Custard Ingredients
425ml/¾ pint whole milk
(warmed not boiling)
3 eggs
3 tbsp brown caster sugar
1 tsp vanilla extract
or ½ tsp vanilla essence
 Butter for greasing
Serve with whipped cream
Serves 4
(3½ litre slow cooker was used.)

Method

1. Set the Slow Cooker to high.
2. Grease 4 ramekins with butter and place 1 tablespoon of golden syrup into each one.
3. Add boiling water to the Crock Pot to about 1inch/2cm high, after checking that the 4 ramekins fit inside the Crock Pot (if not, place a rack or wooden chopsticks between and stack them).
4. Mix the warm milk (I put it in the microwave for 2 minutes), eggs, sugar and vanilla together with a whisk. Put through a sieve and then pour over a spoon into each of the ramekin dishes.
5. Cover tightly with cling film and place in the water using a tin foil lifting strap if necessary. (See Poached Salmon recipe.)
6. Cooking times depend on your Slow Cooker :
   Large/385watt - 45 minutes approx, Medium/285watt - 1 hour approx, Small/160watt - 1 hour 30 minutes approx.
7. As a general rule, when the cling film cover starts to form a dome on the top, the caramel is ready. Take out, allow to cool, then refrigerate and tip out to serve (They taste better the next day.)
8. For variety you can add a teaspoon of instant coffee to the milk to make a coffee caramel. You can replace the golden syrup with apricot jam and serve with whipped cream.

Coconut Rice Pudding with Pineapple

Ingredients

2 x tins 400ml/16fl oz coconut milk
125g/5oz pudding rice
50g/2oz brown sugar
100ml full fat milk
Pinch of grated nutmeg
Serve with sliced, fresh pineapple
Serves 4-6
(3½ litre slow cooker was used.)

Method

1. Set the Slow Cooker to high.
2. Place the coconut milk, pudding rice, brown sugar and milk into the Crock Pot. Mix well and sprinkle with nutmeg.
   Cook on high for 3½ hours with the lid on.
3. Serve with slices of fresh pineapple.
4. You can add a shot of rum to give a different flavour.

For use in a compact oven halve the amount of the ingredients, follow the above cooking method and cook for 35-50 minutes at 153°C (serves 2-3).

Maple and Apple Crumble

Ingredients
2 tbsp maple syrup
2 tbsp brown sugar
1 kg apples (peeled, cored and cubed)
25g/1oz butter
20g/¾oz pecan nuts
Crumble Ingredients
150g/6oz butter
300g/12oz flour
150g/6oz brown sugar
115g (3 slices approx) brown bread crumbs
4 chopped pecan nuts (optional)
Serve with custard.
Serves 4-6
(5½ litre slow cooker was used.)

Method
1. Set the Slow Cooker to high.
2. Add the apples, maple syrup, butter, pecans and brown sugar to the Crock Pot and mix well. Cook for 3 hours with lid on.
3. After this time place the butter, flour, brown sugar and bread (chopped pecans if desired) into a food processor and mix using the mincing blade until a breadcrumb consistency is formed.
4. Place this on top of the stewed fruits, with some pecan nuts and cook for a further hour with the lid on.
5. Remove and serve with custard.

For use with a compact oven place in 2ltr oven dish and cook the fruit and the crumble all at the same time for 50 minutes at 153°C until golden brown (serves 4-6).

109

Poached Pears

Ingredients
6 pears (peeled)
125ml/5fl oz red wine
1 star anise
¼ tsp cinnamon
1 tbsp brown sugar
1 tbsp honey
Garnish
Fresh mint
Serve with mascarpone cheese.
Serves 4-6
(3½ litre slow cooker was used.)

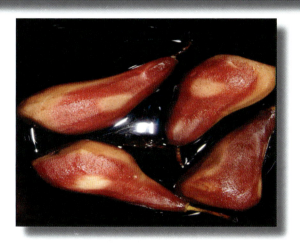

Method

1. Set the Slow Cooker to high.
2. Place the pears, red wine, star anise, cinnamon, brown sugar and honey into the Crock Pot and mix together.
3. Cook for 2 hours with the lid on.
4. Remove and serve with mascarpone cheese and garnish with fresh mint.

For use in a compact oven follow the above cooking method and cook for 45 minutes at 153°C (serves 4-6).

For use in a compact oven follow the cooking method but add 1ltr of boiling water instead of 2ltrs and top up if necessary, and cook for 1 hour at 153°C (serves 4).

Syrup and Pear Sponge Pudding

Ingredients

Base Ingredients
25g/1oz butter
6 tbsp syrup
100g/4oz bread crumbs
2 tbsp water (boiling)

Cake Mix Ingredients
100g/4oz brown caster sugar
100g/4oz self raising flour
2 medium eggs
100g/4oz butter

Filling
1 pear (cored, peeled and finely diced)
Serve with custard or vanilla ice cream.
Serves 4
(6½ litre slow cooker was used.)

Method

1. Place the base ingredients (butter, syrup, breadcrumbs, 2 tbsp boiling water) into a bowl and mix.
2. Add 4 tsp of the pear filling to this mix and stir in well.
3. Butter four ramekins and divide the base ingredients into each one.
4. Place the cake ingredients (sugar, flour, eggs and butter) into a bowl and mix well, add the rest of the diced pear, then divide this mixture into the ramekins.
5. Cover the ramekins with buttered greaseproof paper and secure with tin foil over the top.
6. Place these into the base of the Crock Pot and add 2 litres/80fl oz of boiling water around the ramekins.
7. Cook for 3 hours with the lid on.
8. Serve with custard or vanilla ice cream.

When referring to measurements
As a very rough guide :

tsp = teaspoon
(*heaped slightly unless it's liquid*) 5ml
one teaspoon = ½ dessert spoon
dsp = dessert spoon
(*normally heaped slightly unless it's a liquid*)
one dessert spoon = ½ a tablespoon
tbsp normally = tablespoon
(*heaped slightly unless it's a liquid*)
one tablespoon = two dessert spoons

25g or 1oz is 1 tablespoon of flour (heaped).
25g or 1 oz is 1 tablespoon of sugar (not so heaped).

25g = 1oz
50g = 2 oz
75g = 3 oz
100g = 4 oz
450g = 16 oz = 1lb

150ml = ¼ pint = 5fl oz
300ml = ½ pint = 10fl oz
600ml = 1 pint = 20fl oz
1.1litres = 2 pints = 40fl oz

1cm = ½ inch
2.5cm = 1inch
15cm = 6 inches

All temperatures given are a rough guide, always check the food has been thoroughly cooked before consumption, especially poultry and pork. Always refer to manufacturers instructions as models may vary.